A Benjamin Blog and his Inquisitive Dog Guide

# Wales

Anita Ganeri

Raintree is an imprint of Capstone Global Library Limited, a company incorporated in England and Wales having its registered office at 264 Banbury Road, Oxford, OX2 7DY – Registered company number: 6695582

**www.raintree.co.uk**
myorders@raintree.co.uk

Edited by Helen Cox Cannons
Designed by Philippa Jenkins
Original illustrations © Capstone Global Library Limited 2016
Original map illustration by Oxford Designers and Illustrators
Ben and Barko illustrated by Sernur ISIK
Picture research by Tracy Cummins
Production by Victoria Fitzgerald
Originated by Capstone Global Library Limited
Printed and bound in China

ISBN 978 1 4747 1465 5 (hardback)
19 18 17 16 15
10 9 8 7 6 5 4 3 2 1

ISBN 978 1 4747 1467 9 (paperback)
20 19 18 17
10 9 8 7 6 5 4 3 2

**British Library Cataloguing in Publication Data**
A full catalogue record for this book is available from the British Library.

**Acknowledgements**
We would like to thank the following for permission to reproduce photographs: Alamy: chrisstockphotography, 17, Graham Lawrence, 18, Ian Sheppard, 9, Jeff Morgan, 22, Neil Setchfield, 21, Steve Vidler, 15, travelib, 13; Capstone Press: 5; Getty Images: Bloomberg/Gerallt Llewelyn, 25, Chris Jackson/WPA Pool, 16, Stu Forster, 23; Newscom: Wayne Hutchinson Food and Drink Photos, 24; Shutterstock: Alexander Zavadsky, 28, Fanfo, 20, Gail Johnson, 10, Jane Rix, Cover, Philip Bird LRPS CPAGB, 12, Samot, 7, skyearth, 8, Stephen Meese, 4, Steve Pleydell, 19, 29; SuperStock: Robert Harding Picture Library, 6, Travel Pix Collection/Jon Arnold Images, 14; Thinkstock: acceleratorhams, 27, hipproductions, 26, Matt_Gibson, 11

Some words are shown in bold, **like this**. You can find out what they mean by looking in the glossary.

# Contents

# Welcome to Wales!

Hello! My name's Benjamin Blog and this is Barko Polo, my **inquisitive** dog. (He's named after ancient ace explorer **Marco Polo**.) We have just got back from our latest adventure – exploring Wales. We put this book together from some of the blog posts we wrote on the way.

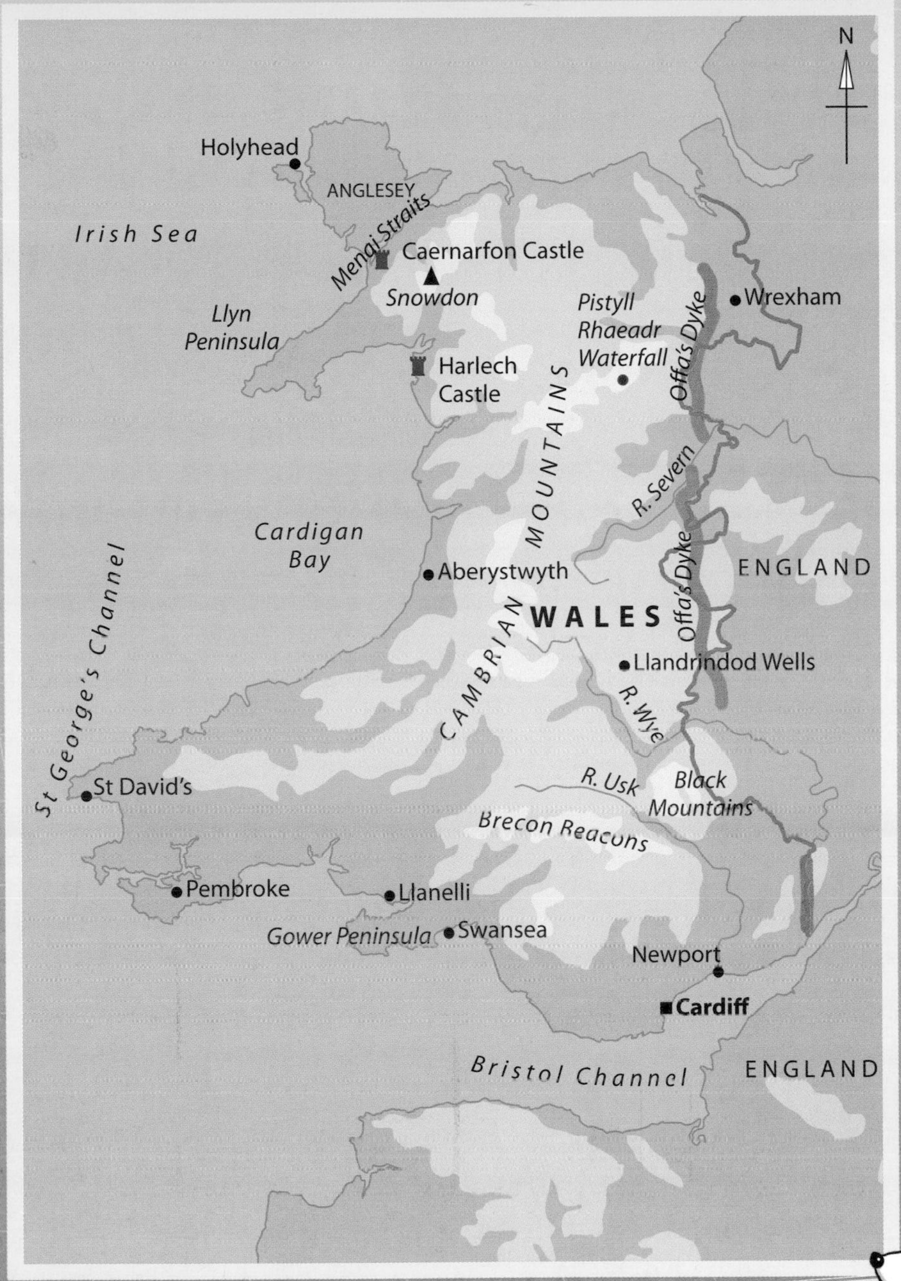
N
Holyhead
ANGLESEY
Menai Straits
Irish Sea
Caernarfon Castle
Snowdon
Llyn Peninsula
Wrexham
Pistyll Rhaeadr Waterfall
Offa's Dyke
Harlech Castle
MOUNTAINS
R. Severn
Cardigan Bay
St George's Channel
Aberystwyth
ENGLAND
WALES
CAMBRIAN
Llandrindod Wells
R. Wye
St David's
R. Usk
Black Mountains
Brecon Beacons
Pembroke
Llanelli
Gower Peninsula
Swansea
Newport
Cardiff
Bristol Channel
ENGLAND

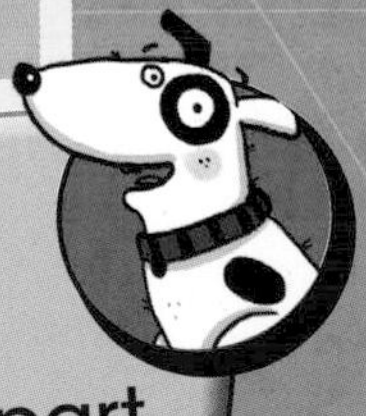

## BARKO'S BLOG-TASTIC WALES FACTS

Wales is a small country in north-west Europe. It is part of the island of Great Britain and one of the countries that make up the United Kingdom. Wales has a long coastline with the Irish Sea (part of the Atlantic Ocean). On land, it is joined to England in the east.

# Forts and castles

Posted by: Ben Blog | 26 June at 16.16 p.m.

We are starting our tour in South Wales at the ancient site of Caerleon. We have come to see a Roman fort here. It was built by the Romans around AD 75 and was home to the Roman army. You can still see the ruins of the soldiers' **barracks**, the **amphitheatre** and baths.

# BARKO'S BLOG-TASTIC WALES FACTS

This is Conwy Castle in North Wales. It was built by the English king Edward I during the 1280s. It was part of a plan by Edward to **conquer** Wales. The castle stands on a rocky ridge, overlooking the river.

I am here!

# Welsh mountains

Posted by: Ben Blog  |  17 July at 2.39 p.m.

From Caerleon, we headed inland to the Brecon Beacons. This National Park has four rugged mountain ranges. The park is very popular with climbers and walkers. I decided to hop on a Welsh mountain pony for a trek.

## BARKO'S BLOG-TASTIC WALES FACTS

Snowdon is the highest mountain in Wales, at 1,085 metres (3,560 feet). It was formed from the ancient rocks from a volcano and carved into shape by **glaciers**. Since 1896, Snowdon Mountain Railway has taken visitors to the top of the mountain.

# Islands and coasts

Posted by: Ben Blog | 23 August at 9.00 a.m.

Our next stop was the island of Anglesey, off the north-west coast of Wales. It's the largest island in Wales and has beautiful beaches and scenery. The Welsh name for Anglesey is "Ynys Môn". I'm here to take part in the Tour de Môn, which is a bicycle race around the island.

# BARKO'S BLOG-TASTIC WALES FACTS

The Gower is a **peninsula** in South Wales. It is famous for its beaches and bays. There are caves around the cliffs. The remains of **prehistoric** people have been found in them.

# City sights

Cardiff is the capital city of Wales. It's a great place to explore. I'm in Cardiff Bay, waiting for a **water bus**. This area used to be the city's docks, where ships loaded up with Welsh coal.
This is a photo I took of the amazing Pierhead Building. It was built in 1896.

Pierhead Building

## BARKO'S BLOG-TASTIC WALES FACTS

St David's is the smallest city in Wales and the whole of the United Kingdom. It is the burial place of St David, the **patron saint** of Wales. You can visit his **shrine** in the cathedral.

# Bore da!

Posted by: Ben Blog | 14 October at 5.23 p.m.

More than 3 million people live in Wales. The most crowded places are cities, such as Cardiff and Swansea, in South Wales. Welsh people are very proud of Wales and Welsh culture. This girl is wearing traditional Welsh dress – a long dress, shawl and tall hat.

## BARKO'S BLOG-TASTIC WALES FACTS

Most people in Wales speak English. Some people also speak Welsh, especially in North and West Wales. Road signs, like this one, are in English and Welsh. In Welsh, "Good morning!" is *Bore da!*

REDUCE
SPEED
NOW

ARAFWCH
NAWR

# Home and school

Posted by: Ben Blog  |  30 November at 8.50 a.m.

In Wales, children start school when they are five years old. Some schools teach the children in Welsh but others teach in both Welsh and English. In all schools, children must learn Welsh until they are 16 years old. I think I might join them for a quick lesson.

**BARKO'S BLOG-TASTIC WALES FACTS**
Today, many Welsh people live in modern houses and flats. But Wales still has many traditional cottages, like this one. This house is made from stone and has a **slate** roof.

# Happy St David's Day!

Posted by: Ben Blog | 1 March at 10.05 a.m.

It's St David's Day! Barko and I are back in Cardiff to celebrate. There's a grand parade through the streets, with dancing red Welsh dragons. People dress up in traditional clothes and carry leeks and daffodils. Leeks and daffodils are two famous symbols of Wales. *Cymru am byth!* (Wales forever!)

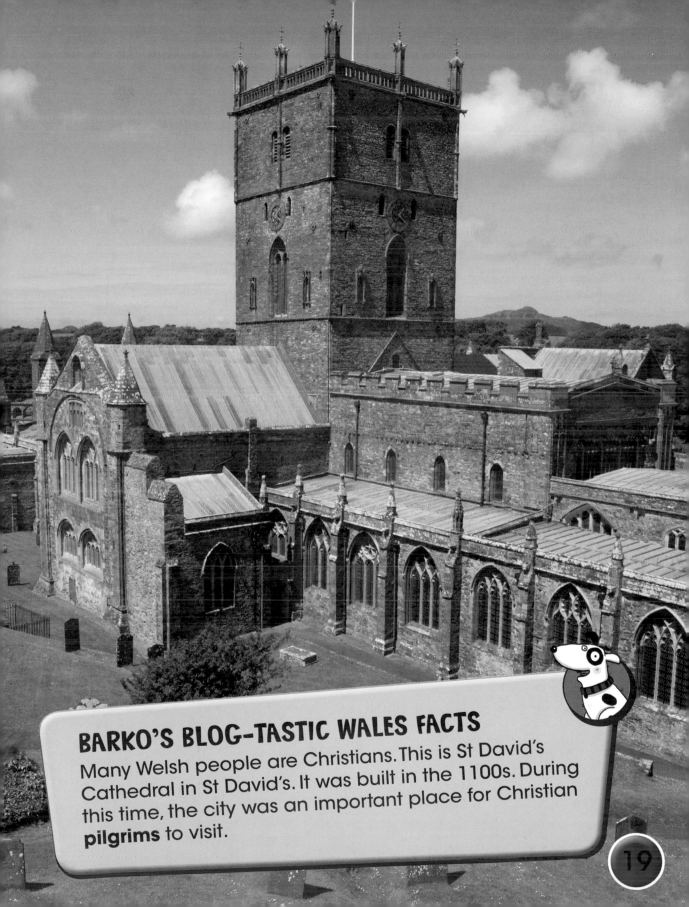

## BARKO'S BLOG-TASTIC WALES FACTS

Many Welsh people are Christians. This is St David's Cathedral in St David's. It was built in the 1100s. During this time, the city was an important place for Christian **pilgrims** to visit.

# Stew and seaweed

Posted by: Ben Blog  |  1 March at 18.38 p.m.

After the parade, Barko and I were hungry. We decided to stop for something to eat. We ordered a bowl of steaming hot cawl. Cawl is a traditional Welsh lamb stew. It has leeks, potatoes, **swedes**, onions and carrots in it. It's delicious but I couldn't eat any more!

**BARKO'S BLOG-TASTIC WALES FACTS**

Laverbread is a bread made from laver. Laver is a type of seaweed. The laver is boiled for several hours, then mashed and rolled in oatmeal. It is fried and eaten with bacon and **cockles** for breakfast.

# Music, poetry and sport

This morning, we arrived in Llanelli for the National Eisteddfod. It's a festival of Welsh music and poetry that is held once a year in different parts of Wales. Winning poets are given a special chair or crown as their prize. I've been working on my poem for weeks.

## BARKO'S BLOG-TASTIC WALES FACTS

Rugby union is a very popular sport in Wales. The Welsh rugby team play at the Millennium Stadium in Cardiff. They are nicknamed the "Red Dragons".

23

# From sheep farms to water power

Posted by: Ben Blog | 29 September at 3.07 p.m.

From Llanelli, Barko and I travelled north again to Snowdonia. We're here to visit a sheep farm. There are more than 9 million sheep in Wales. They are raised for their meat and wool. The farmers use highly trained sheep dogs to round the sheep up. Fancy having a go, Barko?

# BARKO'S BLOG-TASTIC WALES FACTS

This is Dinorwig Power Station in Snowdonia. The power station is hidden inside a mountain. It uses the power of water from a small lake to make electricity. The water flows through tunnels inside the mountain.

# And finally...

For our last stop, we have come to the village of Portmeirion in Cardigan Bay. Portmeirion was built in the 1900s by an architect who liked Italian buildings. There are lots of colourful buildings and squares to explore.

# BARKO'S BLOG-TASTIC WALES FACTS

The Pembrokeshire Coast Path stretches for around 300 kilometres (186 miles) along some of the most breathtaking scenery in the United Kingdom. Thousands of people walk along it every year.

# Wales fact file

Area: 20,782 square kilometres (8,024 square miles)

Population: 3,082,412 (2013)

Capital city: Cardiff

Other main cities and towns: Swansea, Newport, Aberystwyth, Wrexham

Languages: English, Welsh

Main religion: Christianity

Highest mountain: Snowdon (1,085 metres/ 3,560 feet)

Longest river (wholly in Wales): Teifi (122 kilometres/76 miles)

Currency: Pound sterling

# Wales travel quiz

Find out how much you know about Wales with our quick quiz.

1. Which is the highest mountain in Wales?
a) Brecon Beacons
b) Snowdon
c) Everest

2. When is St David's Day?
a) 1 March
b) 2 March
c) 3 March

3. What does *Bore da* mean?
a) Good night
b) Good evening
c) Good morning

4. What is laverbread made from?
a) seaweed
b) volcanic rocks
c) flour

5. What is this?

**Answers**
1. b
2. a
3. c
4. a
5. St David's Cathedral

# Glossary

**amphitheatre**  circular building with rows of seats

**barracks**  buildings where soldiers live

**cockle**  type of shellfish that you can eat

**conquer**  take over a place or people using military force

**glacier**  huge river of ice

**inquisitive**  interested in learning about the world

**Marco Polo**  explorer who lived from about 1254 to 1324; he travelled from Italy to China

**patron saint**  saint who is special to a particular country or place

**peninsula**  narrow strip of land sticking out into the sea from the mainland

**pilgrim**  person who travels to a holy place for religious reasons

**prehistoric**  from a time in the past before things were written down

**shrine**  place where people worship a saint or other holy person

**slate**  type of rock that splits into thin, smooth layers; often used on roofs

**swede**  root vegetable similar to a turnip

**water bus**  boat that takes passengers on a short journey across a river or the sea